JOURNEY TO LONDON
2012 Activity Book
Grades 4-6

© 2012 by Griffin Publishing LLC/United States Olympic Committee

Published by Griffin Publishing LLC under license from the United States Olympic Committee. The use of the Olympic-related marks and terminology is authorized by the United States Olympic Committee pursuant to Title 36 U.S. Code, Section 220506. United States Olympic Committee, One Olympic Plaza, Colorado Springs, CO 80909.

The classroom teacher may reproduce copies of materials in this book for classroom use only. The reproduction of any part for an entire school or school system is strictly prohibited. No part of the publication may be transmitted, stored, or recorded in any form without written permission from Griffin Publishing and Teacher Created Resources.

10 9 8 7 6 5 4 3 2 1

ISBN   1-58000-133-5

TCR   2726

DIRECTOR OF OPERATIONS	Robin L. Howland
WRITER	Karen McRae
EDITOR	Amethyst W. Gaidelis, M.A.
COVER DESIGNER	Brenda DiAntonis
ILLUSTRATOR	Clint McKnight
ART COORDINATOR	Renée Mc Elwee
IMAGING	James Edward Grace, Craig Gunnell

Published in association with and distributed by:

Griffin Publishing LLC

P. O. Box 28627

Santa Ana, CA 92799-8627

www.griffinpublishing.com

Teacher Created Resources

6421 Industry Way

Westminster, CA 92683

www.teachercreated.com

Manufactured in the United States of America

Table of Contents

Meeting Standards 3
Ancient Olympic Games 4
Creating History 5
Modern Olympic Games 6
The Host Cities 8
A Larger Story 10
Welcome to London 11
The Geography of the British Isles 12
Map of the British Isles 13
A Place By Any Other Name 14
The Royal Family 15
The Royal Family Tree 16
Touring London 18
"Site" Seeing 21
Line Through London 22
Where You're Standing 23
Speaking "English" 24
The Torch Relay 26
Olympic Sports 27
The Olympic Program 34
Sports Categories 36
You Make the Choice 37
Olympic Ideals 38
Medal of Honor 39
The Paralympic Games 40
Paralympic Greats 41
The Olympic Mascots 42
The Athlete's Room 43
Five-Day Forecast 44
The Metric System 45
2012 Analogies 46
Keep Track in 2012 47
Answer Key 47

Meeting Standards

The lessons in this book meet the following standards, which are used with permission from McREL (Copyright 2011 McREL, Mid-continent Research for Education and Learning, 4601 DTC Boulevard, Suite 500, Denver, CO 80237. Telephone: 303-377-0990. Website: *www.mcrel.org/standards–benchmarks*).

To align McREL Standards to the Common Core Standards, go to *www.mcrel.org/standards–benchmarks*.

Standards and Benchmarks

GEOGRAPHY

Standard 1. Understands the characteristics and uses of maps, globes, and other geographic tools and technologies

Standard 2. Understands the location of places, geographic features, and patterns of the environment

Standard 3. Understands the characteristics and uses of spatial organization of Earth's surface

HISTORY

Standard 1. (Historical Understanding) Understands and knows how to analyze chronological relationships and patterns

Standard 7. (K–4 History) Understands selected attributes and historical developments of societies in Africa, the Americas, Asia, and Europe

LANGUAGE ARTS

Standard 1. Uses the general skills and strategies of the writing process

Standard 4. Gathers and uses information for research purposes

Standard 5. Uses the general skills and strategies of the reading process

Standard 7. Uses skills and strategies to read a variety of informational texts

MATH

Standard 1. Uses a variety of strategies in the problem-solving process

Standard 2. Understands and applies basic and advanced properties of the concepts of numbers

Standard 3. Uses basic and advanced procedures while performing the processes of computation

Standard 4. Understands and applies basic and advanced properties of the concepts of measurement

Standard 5. Understands and applies basic and advanced properties of the concepts of geometry

Standard 6. Understands and applies basic and advanced concepts of statistics and data analysis

Standard 8. Understands and applies basic and advanced properties of the functions and algebra

Ancient Olympic Games

Before we look ahead to the 2012 Olympic Games, it is important to look back and learn about how it all began. Can you guess how long it has been since the first Olympic Games were played? 100 years? 1,000 years? Actually, it happened way back in 776 BCE, exactly 2,788 years ago.

The Ancient Olympic Games did not look much like the global event we celebrate today. For instance, in the very beginning, there was only one event! It was called the *stadion*, and it was a running race that covered a distance of 180–240 meters (about 200–260 yards). By comparison, the 2012 Olympic Games will feature 302 events. Also, in 776 BCE, only free men who spoke Greek were allowed to compete. In contrast, the 2012 Games will bring together athletes from more than 200 countries.

These Ancient Games were held every *olympiad*—the name for a period of four years—until 393 CE when they were outlawed for religious reasons by Roman Emperor Theodosius I. They did not begin again until the Modern Olympic Games were established in 1896.

Directions: Your teacher is going to read aloud several statements about the Olympic Games. After hearing each statement, do the following:

- ✦ If you think the statement is only true about the *Ancient* Olympic Games, raise your left hand.
- ✦ If you think it is only true about the *Modern* Olympic Games, raise your right hand.
- ✦ If you think the statement is true about *both* the Ancient Games and the Modern Games, raise both of your hands.

1. The winner receives an olive wreath.
2. The winner receives a gold medal.
3. The athletes use equipment designed with the help of computer technology.
4. Boxers sometimes put metal in their hard leather gloves.
5. Women compete in more than 100 events.
6. The athletes wear almost no clothing.
7. Fifteen new venues were built especially for the Games.
8. The Games are held every four years.
9. The Games are often held in Asia and North America.
10. An Olympic Truce is enacted so that athletes can travel safely from their countries to the Games.

Creating History

The further you go back in history, the more difficult it is to know if the stories we hear are truth (they did happen that way) or myth (they didn't quite happen that way, or they didn't even happen at all!). News of what happened and how it happened was spread by word of mouth, and sometimes not everything that was spread was true.

Even though we now have the ability to capture events on film, the spread of information by "word of mouth" has been taken to a whole new level—and a whole new speed. With our advanced technology, information can travel instantly from person to person and from group to group.

Directions: The myths below have been told about some of the legendary athletes who competed in the Ancient Olympic Games. Pretend that texting and social media existed back then and that you were there to witness and report on these incredible achievements. Retell one event for each athlete, using 140 characters (letters, spaces, etc.) or fewer. Use your own language, as if you were reporting the events to your friends. And remember, the tales you tell will be passed on to future generations who will never see the sights you have seen or know what really happened.

1. **Milo of Croton**—This wrestler won six Olympic competitions. He was known for his strong wrists and hands. It was said that he would show his strength by holding out his hands with his fingers spread out. No man could even bend his little finger.

   _____

   _____

   _____

2. **Melankomas of Caria**—This boxer was known for his handsome body and good looks. His boxing style was to spend the entire fight avoiding the blows of his opponents. He wouldn't throw any punches himself! He was so quick that no one ever hit him. His opponents got so tired and frustrated that they gave up.

   _____

   _____

   _____

3. **Astylos of Croton**—This Olympic hero won running events in three straight Olympic Games. He became a hated man, though, when he accepted money to compete for a different city than his hometown of Croton. The citizens of Croton kicked him out of their city and destroyed the statue of him that once stood there.

   _____

   _____

   _____

Another Idea: On the back of this paper, write a myth about an athlete or celebrity from today. Have fun exaggerating their skills or beauty. What amazing feats did your person accomplish? Why should this person be remembered for thousands of years? Try to not use the person's name, so your classmates can guess who you have written about.

Modern Olympic Games

During the 19th century, people became interested in the Ancient Olympic Games that had taken place centuries earlier. Several small Olympic-style festivals were held with athletic competitions. The large-scale event that we now know of as the Olympic Games, however, did not take root until the 1890s when a French teacher and historian named Pierre de Coubertin studied the Ancient Games. He wanted to get the youth of the world competing in sports instead of fighting in wars, and he felt that a modern version of the Olympic Games was a way to accomplish this goal.

In 1894, de Coubertin founded the International Olympic Committee (IOC). The committee members met and debated how to put his plan into action. They planned to begin this new Olympic tradition in 1896 in Greece, the country where it all began. They also decided that in future years, the Games should be hosted by different countries throughout the world. This idea gave many countries a chance to see this international event up close.

Pierre de Coubertin

The 1896 Olympic Games were held in Athens, Greece, from April 6 to April 15. Athletes from 14 nations competed in just nine sports: athletics, cycling, fencing, gymnastics, shooting, swimming, tennis, weightlifting, and wrestling. Here are some of the highlights of the 1896 Games:

- A Greek athlete named Spyridon Louis became a national hero when he won the marathon race.

- American brothers John Paine and Sumner Paine became the first relatives to come in first place in Olympic events when they each won a shooting event.

- A Greek athlete named Stamata Revithi was told that she could not compete in the Games because she was a woman. As a sign of protest, she ran the complete marathon course the day after the men had.

Many things have changed in the 116 years since those first Modern Olympic Games. The Olympic Games expanded to become a global event. In 2012, more than 10,000 men and women from over 200 nations will compete in 26 different sports. Some other changes are as follows:

- The Games went from an all-male event to a more inclusive one. Women were allowed to compete on a limited basis by 1900. In 1984, the women's marathon became an official event. By the 2008 Olympic Games, all but two countries—Saudi Arabia and Qatar—that regularly compete in the Games had sent female athletes to represent them.

- The medals awarded to the winners changed in 1904 to gold (first place), silver (second place), and bronze (third place). Prior to that year, the first- and second-place winners received silver and bronze metals.

Modern Olympic Games

Directions: Use the information on page 6 to complete these challenges.

Bronze-Medal Challenge

Give the names and nationalities of the people who fit the descriptions below.

	Description	Name(s)	Nationality
a.	first pair of brothers to win first-place Olympic medals		
b.	first athlete to win the first-place Olympic medal in the marathon		
c.	founder of the International Olympic Committee		

Silver-Medal Challenge

Put these events in time order. Write a "1" by the event that happened first in history, a "2" by the event that happened second, and so on.

_____ The bronze medal was given to athletes who finished in third place.

_____ The Ancient Olympic Games took place.

_____ A woman won an Olympic gold medal in a marathon race.

_____ Pierre de Coubertin started the International Olympic Committee.

_____ Two brothers won gold medals in the same Olympic Games.

Gold-Medal Challenge

It's an Olympic scavenger hunt! Find the following items in the article on the Modern Olympic Games. There may be more than one item to be found, but you only need to list one.

a. a country that begins with "Q"	**d.** a five-digit number
b. a compound word	**e.** a five-syllable word
c. a hyphenated word	**f.** a synonym of the word "discussed"

The Host Cities

Year	Olympiad	Opening Ceremonies	Closing Ceremonies	Host City	Host Country
1896	I	April 6	April 15	Athens	Greece
1900	II	May 14	October 28	Paris	France
1904	III	July 1	November 23	St. Louis, MO	United States
1908	IV	April 27	October 31	London	England
1912	V	May 5	July 27	Stockholm	Sweden
1920	VII	April 20	September 12	Antwerp	Belgium
1924	VIII	May 4	July 27	Paris	France
1928	IX	July 28	August 12	Amsterdam	The Netherlands
1932	X	July 30	August 14	Los Angeles, CA	United States
1936	XI	August 1	August 16	Berlin	Germany
1948	XIV	July 29	August 14	London	England
1952	XV	July 19	August 3	Helsinki	Finland
1956	XVI	November 22	December 8	Melbourne	Australia
1960	XVII	August 25	September 11	Rome	Italy
1964	XVIII	October 10	October 24	Tokyo	Japan
1968	XIX	October 12	October 27	Mexico City	Mexico
1972	XX	August 26	September 11	Munich	Germany
1976	XXI	July 17	August 1	Montreal	Canada
1980	XXII	July 19	August 3	Moscow	Soviet Union (USSR)
1984	XXIII	July 28	August 12	Los Angeles, CA	United States
1988	XXIV	September 17	October 2	Seoul	South Korea
1992	XXV	July 25	August 9	Barcelona	Spain
1996	XXVI	July 19	August 4	Atlanta, GA	United States
2000	XXVII	September 15	October 1	Sydney	Australia
2004	XXVIII	August 13	August 29	Athens	Greece
2008	XXIX	August 8	August 24	Beijing	China
2012	XXX	July 27	August 12	London	England
2016	XXXI	August 5	August 21	Rio de Janeiro	Brazil

The Host Cities

Directions: Use the chart on page 8 to complete these challenges.

Bronze-Medal Challenge

On three occasions in history, the Olympic Games began on the same date. On the first line of the diagram, write that date. On the other three lines, write the years in which the Olympic Games began on that date.

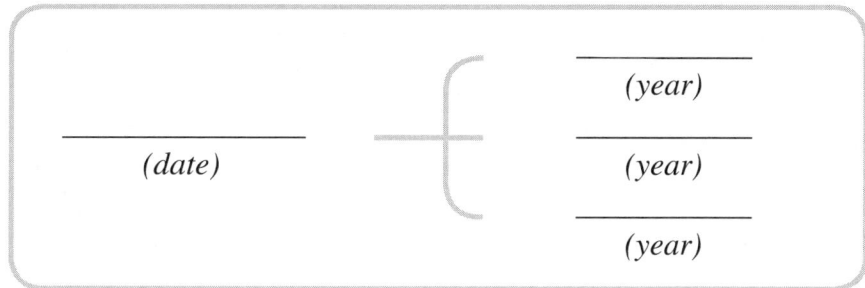

Silver-Medal Challenge

Answer the following questions. Use complete sentences.

1. In which year did the Olympic Games begin at the latest date in the calendar year? (Include the day and month in your answer.)

2. Using all of the information provided, give a logical reason why the warm-weather Games began on such a late date in this year.

Gold-Medal Challenge

When the 2016 Olympic Games are held in Rio de Janeiro, it will mark the first time the Games have been played on the continent of South America. Look at the pie chart. Write the letter of the appropriate section on the line to the left of the matching continent. Hint: While much of the Soviet Union was in Asia, Moscow was (and is) in Europe.

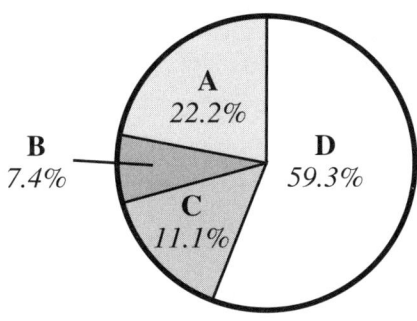

Percentage of Olympiads on Each Continent

Letter	Continent
	Asia
	Australia
	Europe
	North America

A Larger Story

The events that will take place between July 27, 2012, and August 12, 2012, will become part of a larger story. Some olympiads are memorable because of legendary athletes. Others are defined by the world events that surrounded them. There are even a few that were scheduled to take place but did not.

Directions: Follow these steps to learn more about the Olympic Games of the past.

Step 1: Write the day of the month on which you were born.
(Example: "15" if you were born on April 15th)   _____

Step 2: Write your answer to question 1 in roman numerals.
(Example: "XV" for 15)   _____

Step 3: Use an Internet search engine to research your Olympic Games. Type in the number of your Games followed by the phrase "Olympic Games Summer." (Example: If your birthday is on the 15th, type in "XV Olympic Games Summer")

Step 4: Complete the form below.

Your olympiad (in roman numeral form): _____

The year the Games were held (or were supposed to be held): _____

The host city where the Games were held (or were supposed to be held):
_____

✦ Were the Games held that year? (Circle one)   YES   NO

If you answered "YES," complete the following:

✦ How many nations competed in these Games? _____

✦ Who were the stars of these Games? Describe at least two athletes and their accomplishments.
_____
_____
_____

If you answered "NO," complete the following:

✦ Why were they not held? Write at least one complete sentence to support your answer.
_____
_____
_____

✦ Did that city host another Olympic Games at some point? If so, give the year. _____

Welcome to London

Welcome to London, the capital of England and of the United Kingdom, as well. When traveling to this historic city, a visitor would most likely arrive at London Heathrow Airport. The Heathrow Airport handles more international travelers than any other airport in the world. From there, tourists are encouraged to visit some of the city's many historical sites. And any destination within the city can be reached easily in one of London's famous black cabs or by a quick trip on the Tube. The 2012 Olympic Games will not just be about sports and the athletes who compete in them; they will also be about experiencing new peoples, places, and cultures.

While this will be a record-breaking third time that London has hosted the Olympic Games, it will be the first time since 1948. Everything has grown more intense since then—from the media coverage to the athletic competition—and expectations are higher than ever. These days, tens of thousands of athletes, spectators, and media members flock to the Olympic Games.

Think about the things London will need to be a good host for all of those people who will attend and participate in the games. Think about the things an event of this size would need and consider the ways a city could be prepared or unprepared to fulfill those needs. Fill out the chart with as many details as you can think of.

What is Needed	Why This is Needed	Well Prepared	Not Prepared
Housing			
Stadiums/Venues			
Transportation			
Volunteers			

Answer the following questions on the back of this page. Explain your answers.
- Would your city be a good host for the Olympic Games?
- Would it be a better host for the Olympic Winter Games?

To see how London is preparing for the 2012 Olympic Games, visit the official website at *www.london2012.com* and click on the "Making it happen" tab.

The Geography of the British Isles

Directions: Read each description to learn more about the countries and bodies of water in and around the British Isles. Then, cut out the map labels and paste them into the correct spaces on the map on page 13. Use an atlas or the Internet to help you.

England	Nearly 80% of the population of the British Isles lives in **England**. London, the host of the 2012 Olympic Games, is England's capital city.
Wales	The site of some Olympic football (soccer) matches in 2012, **Wales** shares the island of Great Britain with England and Scotland.
Scotland	Located to the north of England, **Scotland** will also host Olympic football (soccer) matches in the summer of 2012.
Northern Ireland	Along with England, Scotland, and Wales, **Northern Ireland** is one of the four countries that make up the United Kingdom.
Republic of Ireland	Spanning nearly 5/6 of the island of Ireland, the **Republic of Ireland** officially gained complete independence from the United Kingdom in 1949.
Atlantic Ocean	The world's second-largest ocean (and its saltiest), the **Atlantic Ocean** covers a huge area of Earth to the west of Great Britain and Ireland.
English Channel	The **English Channel** is a narrow waterway that separates Great Britain from northern France.
River Thames	The **River Thames** (pronounced "temms") flows through central London and into the North Sea. It has provided water, food, and transportation to southern England for thousands of years.

Map of the British Isles

Paste the labels from page 12 in the appropriate spaces on the map of England below.

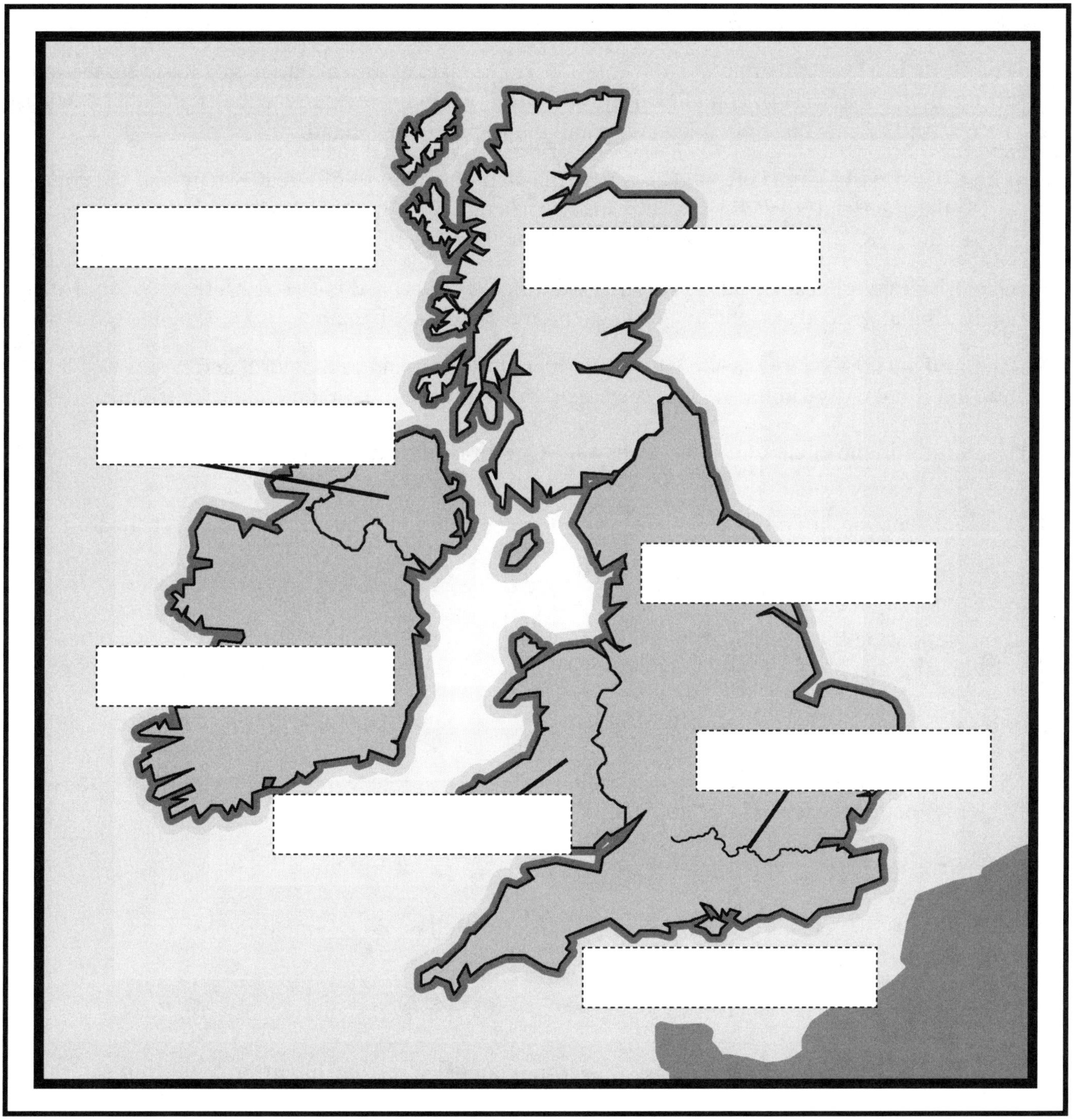

A Place By Any Other Name

The geography of England and its surrounding area can be a bit confusing. There are many names for the many regions. Here are a few things to remember. (Look at a map for reference.)

✦ **The British Isles**—This refers to the entire group of islands and countries that make up the land off the northwest coast of continental Europe. The two main sovereign (free) states that comprise the British Isles are the United Kingdom and the Republic of Ireland.

✦ **The United Kingdom (U.K.)**—This sovereign state includes all of Great Britain and the country of Northern Ireland, as well as several smaller islands in the region. Northern Ireland is the only part of the U.K. that shares a land border with another sovereign state (Ireland).

✦ **Great Britain**—Great Britain is the largest European island and is also the largest of the British Isles. England, Scotland, and Wales make up most of Great Britain.

✦ **England**—This Olympic host country is bordered by Scotland to the north and Wales to the west. London, England's capital, is also the capital of and largest city in the United Kingdom.

Directions: Fill in the circle of each true answer. Questions may have more than one right answer.

1. You are standing in Trafalgar Square, a popular destination in Central London. Where are you?
   Ⓐ British Isles Ⓑ United Kingdom Ⓒ Great Britain Ⓓ England

2. You are kissing the Blarney Stone while on vacation in the Republic of Ireland. Legend has it that kissing this block of bluestone will make you an eloquent speaker. Where are you?
   Ⓐ British Isles Ⓑ United Kingdom Ⓒ Great Britain Ⓓ England

3. You are standing in a public square in Edinburgh, Scotland, listening to the mournful sounds of bagpipes being played. Where are you?
   Ⓐ British Isles Ⓑ United Kingdom Ⓒ Great Britain Ⓓ England

4. You are part of a crowd watching a red panda eat at Belfast Zoo, located in the capital of Northern Ireland. Where are you?
   Ⓐ British Isles Ⓑ United Kingdom Ⓒ Great Britain Ⓓ England

5. You are carrying the flag and representing your country at the Opening Ceremonies of the 2012 Olympic Games. Where are you?
   Ⓐ British Isles Ⓑ United Kingdom Ⓒ Great Britain Ⓓ England

The Royal Family

The British monarchy has been an important part of the British government for thousands of years. (A monarchy is a type of government with one ruler.) Until the 19th century, the British monarchs made and passed the laws of the land. Since then, however, the monarchy has become a constitutional monarchy, meaning the ruler no longer has the power to pass laws. Now, Parliament makes and passes the laws, headed by the Prime Minister. It is the elected governmental body, much like Congress in the United States. The British monarch remains politically neutral in both ceremonial and official duties, meaning that he or she doesn't take sides. In this way, the monarch provides the nation with a strong and unified national front.

The current British monarch is *Queen Elizabeth II*, the eldest daughter of King George VI and Queen Elizabeth I. Elizabeth II ascended to the throne in 1952. Along with the Royal Family—her closest relatives—the Queen performs many ceremonial duties and supports many charitable causes.

Over recent years, the British Royal Family's lives have been followed by people all over the world. Here are a few of their most memorable moments:

- **July 29, 1981**—*Lady Diana Frances Spencer* married *Prince Charles*, the eldest son of Queen Elizabeth II. The world watched this fairy tale wedding unfold as Diana, looking every bit the princess she was about to become, walked down the aisle in a diamond tiara and a silk-taffeta dress with a 25-foot train.

- **June 21, 1982**—Princess Diana gave birth to *William Arthur Philip Louis*. As Prince Charles's first son, William instantly became second in line behind his father as heir to the throne.

- **September 6, 1997**—Widespread grief and devastation were felt as Diana, only 36 years old, died in a car accident on August 31, 1997. Britain (and, in large part, the world) had grown to love Diana. She was called "the people's princess" and was looked up to for her tireless efforts on behalf of many charities. On September 6, she was laid to rest in a funeral attended by over 2,000 people and viewed on British TV by over 32 million people.

- **April 29, 2011**—*Prince William*, eldest son of Prince Charles and Princess Diana, married *Catherine "Kate" Middleton* in a much anticipated and much celebrated wedding extravaganza. An estimated audience of 2.5 billion people (on TV and online) followed the ceremony with awe and admiration as the future king married his college sweetheart. On that day, Kate went from being a commoner—a person without royal bloodlines—to becoming "Her Royal Highness."

> **Activity:** On a separate piece of paper, write an essay about your country's head of state. Do you have a king or queen who has inherited the throne, or do you have a leader who was elected by the people? Give the pros and cons of Britain's or your country's system.

The Royal Family Tree

The British Royal Family that we know today descended from a long line of royalty. In order to keep track of the history of any family—royal or not—a family tree can be drawn. A family tree is a simple diagram that shows the relationships of family members down through the years.

Directions: Below is one part of the British Royal Family's family tree. Look it over, and then complete the activity at the bottom of the page. You will also use this family tree to complete the activity on page 17.

Victoria (1819–1901) — no siblings
Reign: June 20, 1837–January 22, 1901
Married: Prince Albert

Edward VII (1841–1910) — 3 brothers & 5 sisters
Reign: January 22, 1901–May 6, 1910
Married: Princess Alexandra

George V (1865–1936) — 2 brothers & 3 sisters
Reign: May 6, 1910–January 20, 1936
Married: Princess Mary

Edward VIII (1894–1972) — 3 brothers & 1 sister
Reign: January 20, 1936
 –December 11, 1936
Married: Wallis Simpson

George VI (1895–1952)
Reign: December 11, 1936
 –February 6, 1952
Married: Lady Elizabeth

Elizabeth II (1926–) — 1 sister
Reign: February 6, 1952–present
Married: Philip, Duke of Edinburgh

Prince Charles (1948–) — 2 brothers & 1 sister
Married: Lady Diana Spencer (divorced)

Prince William (1982–)
Married: Catherine Middleton

Prince Henry (1984–)

Activity: On a separate piece of paper, create a family tree for your family. Ask your parents, grandparents, aunts, and uncles to help you recreate your family's history. Go as far back as you can. Because every family is different, every family tree will be different also.

Another Idea: Create a family tree of one of your country's leaders (president, etc.).

The Royal Family Tree

Directions: Use the information on pages 15 and 16 to complete these challenges.

Bronze-Medal Challenge

Put these British monarchs in order from 1–6 by how long their reign was or has been. Put a "1" next to the monarch with the longest reign. Put a "6" next to the monarch who had the shortest reign. Note: Make sure you are looking at the ruler's reign and not the years he or she was alive.

_____ Victoria

_____ Edward VII

_____ George V

_____ Edward VIII

_____ George VI

_____ Elizabeth II

Silver-Medal Challenge

Draw lines to match the husband or wife to the correct member of the Royal Family.

Diana Spencer	George VI
Wallis Simpson	Prince Charles
Catherine Middleton	Prince William
Lady Elizabeth	Edward VIII
Prince Albert	Queen Victoria

Gold-Medal Challenge

Solve the equations.

1. [number of children Victoria had] **x** [number of siblings George V had]

   Answer: _____

2. [answer to #1] **−** [George VI's age when he began his reign]

   Answer: _____

3. [answer to #2] **+** [Prince William's age when the 2012 Olympic Games begin]

   Answer: _____

Touring London

The Old . . .

London has been a major settlement for over 2,000 years. A city that old is bound to be full of historical places of interest. Here are a few popular tourist destinations:

The Tower of London is a historic castle built in the 11th century on the bank of the River Thames in central London. The Tower is actually a complex of several buildings surrounded by defensive walls and a moat. Throughout London's history, those who controlled this stronghold often controlled the city. The Tower is also infamous for serving as a prison and place of torture for several centuries. Since 1303, and to this day, the Crown Jewels of the United Kingdom have been housed in the Tower. Along with the nearby **Tower Bridge** (built in the late 19th century), the Tower receives throngs of tourists each day.

London Tower Bridge

Westminster Palace, or the **Houses of Parliament**, is also situated along the River Thames. This building was originally built in medieval times but was greatly destroyed by huge fires in both 1512 and 1834. The palace was rebuilt in the mid-19th century. It is where the two house of Parliament meet to make laws. The famous **Clock Tower**, better known as **Big Ben**, rises above the north end of the palace. The clock sits near the top of a 316-foot (96.3 m) tower and has a minute hand that is 14 feet (4.3 m) long. Since it began working in 1859, the reliable clock has struck every hour within a second.

The Monument in London is the tallest column of stone in the world. It was built in the 1670s to commemorate the Great Fire of London, which burned for four days in 1666 and destroyed much of London. The Monument is 202 feet (61.57 m) high, the exact distance from the Monument to the bakery where the fire started. Visitors can climb the 311 narrow winding steps inside the Monument to reach the viewing platform at the top.

Buckingham Palace has been the official residence of the British monarch since 1837. It was built in 1705 and has been greatly enlarged over the years. The Royal Family often entertains official visitors in this palace. For a fee, tourists can get a look inside the Palace's history-filled halls. In the courtyard outside, tourists often line up to get a free view of the **Changing of the Queen's Guard**. At 11:30 a.m. each day in the summer (and every other day in the winter), the soldiers in charge of guarding the Palace change units. In a 45-minute ceremony involving a full military band, the New Guard comes in and the Old Guard goes out.

Go to page 19 to continue reading more about London's famous historical sites. Then, take the "Touring London" challenge on page 20.

Touring London

...And the New

It might be a stretch to call the **London Underground** new, because the "Tube" (as it's called by Londoners) is the oldest underground railway system in the world. The first sections of the Tube were opened in 1863, and electric operation began in 1890. Today, the Tube's network of tracks spans 250 miles (402 km) in, around, and mostly under Greater London. Its well-designed map has become the model for subway systems around the world, and its bullseye logo is instantly recognizable throughout the city.

The **Channel Tunnel** (or "Chunnel" as it's often called) is possibly an even more impressive feat of engineering. This 31.4-mile (50.5 km) rail tunnel runs from southern England to northern France. It was completed in 1994. What makes this impressive is that a large body of water—the English Channel—separates these two countries. Over 23 miles (almost 38 km) of the Chunnel actually runs under the sea! It took 6 years and cost $11 billion (4.6 billion British pounds) to construct, but a high-speed train trip from London to Paris now takes just over two hours.

The **London Eye**, the most popular paid tourist attraction in London, sits along the River Thames. It is also called the Millennium Wheel, because it opened on December 31, 1999. At that time, it was the largest Ferris wheel in the world. It is 443 feet (135 m) tall! Passengers can enjoy breathtaking views of London while riding in one of 32 sealed capsules. Each capsule can hold 25 people at one time.

The **Shard London Bridge Building** will be completed by the time of the 2012 Olympic Games. Nicknamed "The Shard," this enormous skyscraper will immediately become the tallest building in Western Europe. But its height is not all that will make it special and unique. The entire surface of this building will be covered in glass. The glazing and placement of each glass pane will be designed to reflect the changing patterns in the sky.

Shard London Bridge Building

And no discussion of "New" London would be complete without a mention of **Olympic Park**. This newly constructed complex in East London will feature seven new sports venues and an Olympic Village, all built in preparation for the 2012 Games.

Activity: If you were visiting London, which of the attractions listed on pages 18–19 would you rush to see first? On a separate piece of paper, list the three London landmarks you found most interesting. Write a paragraph explaining your choices.

Touring London

Directions: Use the information on pages 18 and 19 to complete these challenges.

Bronze-Medal Challenge

Fill in the circle next to the math equation that would be used to answer the question. On the line next to the correct equation, write the value of x.

Question: How many people could ride the London Eye at one time?

Ⓐ 443 + 32 = x _____   Ⓒ 443 ÷ 32 = x _____

Ⓑ 32 + 25 = x _____   Ⓓ 32 x 25 = x _____

Silver-Medal Challenge

Look at the timeline. The letters A, B, C, and D represent the events listed below. Next to each event, write the letter from the timeline that it corresponds to.

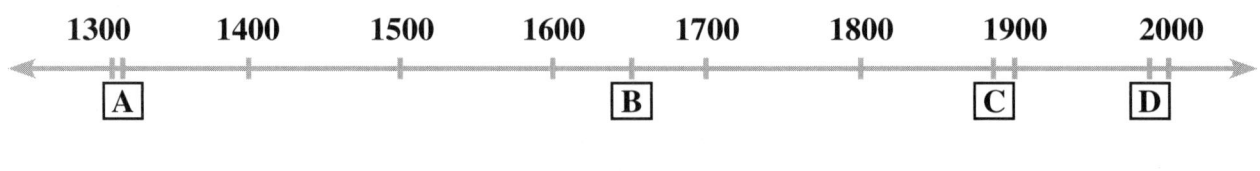

_____ The world's first underground electric trains begin operating.

_____ The Great Fire of London begins in a bakery and destroys much of the city.

_____ Work is completed on an underwater tunnel between England and France.

_____ The Crown Jewels are first kept in the location in which they remain to this day.

Gold-Medal Challenge

Look at the heights of the three boxes below. If, based on their heights, each box represents a London landmark, which landmark does Box A stand for? Circle your answer and explain.

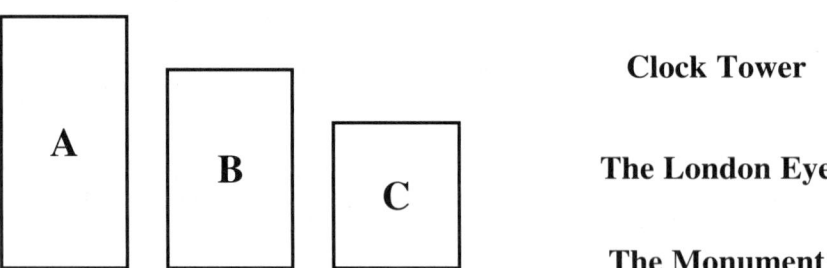

Clock Tower

The London Eye

The Monument

Explanation: _____

_____

20

"Site" Seeing

Because of the Internet, it has become faster and easier to see sights you may never have seen, in faraway places you may never get to visit. With a few clicks, you can see the world in vivid detail.

Directions: Read each question carefully to discover what is being asked about various landmarks around London. Then, click on the "Images" tab on a search-engine website (Google, Yahoo!, etc.) to find pictures. Enter the specific search term given to ensure that you get the best images possible.

Teacher Note: Be sure to monitor students during this activity. Set the search engine's controls to "Safe" or "Strict" and make sure that the search terms given do not yield any inappropriate results.

Landmark	Search Term	Question	Your Answer
Buckingham Palace	"Changing of the Queen's Guard"	What colors are the hats and coats worn by the Queen's Guards?	Hats: _____ Coats: _____
The London Eye	"London Eye Capsules"	What object does a capsule (the place where people ride) on the London Eye *most* resemble?	Ⓐ an eyeball Ⓑ a pea pod Ⓒ a jelly bean Ⓓ a rocket
The London Underground	"London Tube Symbol"	What does the symbol found at stops along the London Underground (the "Tube") look like?	*Draw your answer.*
Shakespeare's Globe Theater	"Shakespeare's Globe Theater Interior"	How many seating tiers does the theater have?	_____
The Shard	"London Shard Building"	What geometric shape does the Shard London Bridge Building *most* resemble?	Ⓐ a sphere Ⓑ a pyramid Ⓒ a cylinder Ⓓ a cube

Line Through London

If you visit the Royal Observatory in Greenwich, a district in Southeast London, you can actually stand in two different parts of the world at the same time. That is because there is a very special strip of stainless steel running through the observatory's courtyard. Stand on one side, and you are in Earth's Western Hemisphere; stand on the other, and you are in the Eastern Hemisphere. Stand with one foot on each side of the line, and you are in both. This line divides Earth in half from top to bottom. It is called the Prime Meridian.

For centuries, people have worked to map Earth. Two types of lines were drawn to divide the world into sections. Longitude lines were drawn from north to south, while latitude lines were drawn from east to west. Longitude lines (also called meridians) can be used to determine a place's east-west position on Earth's surface. Latitude lines are used to determine a place's north-south position.

The line of latitude that goes around the middle of Earth is the Equator. It is an equal distance from both the North Pole and the South Pole. Just like the Prime Meridian divides the Eastern and Western Hemispheres, the Equator divides Earth into Northern and Southern Hemispheres.

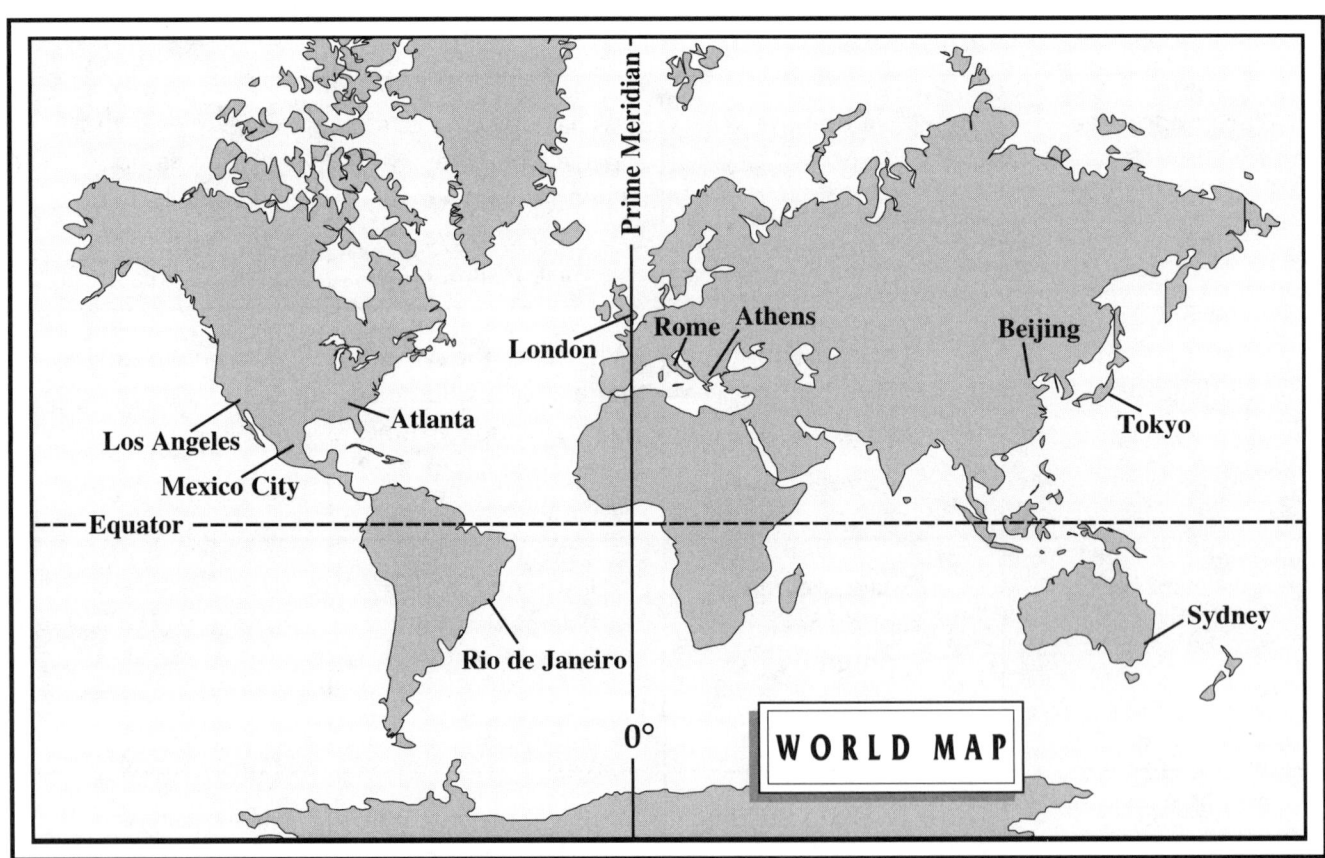

Use the information and the map above to complete the "Where You're Standing" activity on page 23.

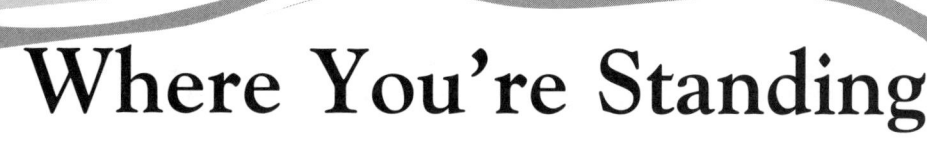

Where You're Standing

Directions: Imagine you are standing in the Olympic host cities named below. For each one, fill in the circle of the hemisphere you could be standing in. Each location will be in two hemispheres, and one will be in there. Use the information from page 22 to help you.

1. Athens, Greece (Olympiads I and XXVIII)   Ⓐ Northern   Ⓑ Southern   Ⓒ Western   Ⓓ Eastern
2. Los Angeles, California, United States (Olympiads X and XXIII)   Ⓐ Northern   Ⓑ Southern   Ⓒ Western   Ⓓ Eastern
3. Rome, Italy (Olympiad XVII)   Ⓐ Northern   Ⓑ Southern   Ⓒ Western   Ⓓ Eastern
4. Sydney, Australia (Olympiad XXVII)   Ⓐ Northern   Ⓑ Southern   Ⓒ Western   Ⓓ Eastern
5. Mexico City, Mexico (Olympiad XIX)   Ⓐ Northern   Ⓑ Southern   Ⓒ Western   Ⓓ Eastern
6. Tokyo, Japan (Olympiad XVIII)   Ⓐ Northern   Ⓑ Southern   Ⓒ Western   Ⓓ Eastern
7. Atlanta, Georgia, United States (Olympiad XXVI)   Ⓐ Northern   Ⓑ Southern   Ⓒ Western   Ⓓ Eastern
8. Beijing, China (Olympiad XXIX)   Ⓐ Northern   Ⓑ Southern   Ⓒ Western   Ⓓ Eastern
9. Rio de Janeiro, Brazil (Olympiad XXXI)   Ⓐ Northern   Ⓑ Southern   Ⓒ Western   Ⓓ Eastern
10. London, England (Olympiad XXX)   Ⓐ Northern   Ⓑ Southern   Ⓒ Western   Ⓓ Eastern

Speaking "English"

The English language is one of the most important and influential languages on the planet. Consider these facts:

- English is the language with the third most native speakers in the world. (Mandarin Chinese and Spanish have the most and second most, respectively.)

- English is the official language of over 50 countries, more than any other language.

- English is the leading language of international discourse—in other words, talks between nations.

While it's true that the United States and Great Britain use English as their primary language, it would not be true to say that every English word means the same thing or is spelled the same way in the two countries. Below left is a list of things that are called one thing in England (British English) and something else entirely in the United States (American English). Below right is a list of words that are spelled differently in each country.

Say What?	
American English	**British English**
apartment	flat
cookie	biscuit
elevator	lift
garbage man	dustman
gasoline	petrol
guy	bloke
hood (of car)	bonnet
mom	mum
policeman	bobby
argument	row
soccer	football
trash	rubbish
truck	lorry
vacation	holiday

Spelled How?	
American English	**British English**
airplane	aeroplane
analyze	analyse
center	centre
color	colour
cruelest	cruellest
favorite	favourite
gray	grey
honor	honour
organize	organise
program	programme
realize	realise
theater	theatre
ton	tonne
traveler	traveller

Speaking "English"

Directions: Use the information provided on page 24 to complete these challenges.

Bronze-Medal Challenge

In Column A, put the three world languages with the most native speakers in order by how many people speak them. In Column B, write the same three languages in alphabetical order.

Column A	Column B
_____	_____
_____	_____
_____	_____

Silver-Medal Challenge

Next to each definition, write the matching word from the "Spelled How?" list on page 24. Use the clue in parentheses to choose the correct spelling.

1. one who goes from place to place (British) _____
2. meanest, most hurtful (American) _____
3. place where actors work (British) _____
4. red, blue, purple, green, etc. (British) _____
5. to put things in order (American) _____

Gold-Medal Challenge

Read the following story. Using words from the "Say What?" list on page 24, rewrite the story, substituting British English for American English. There are 10 words that need to be changed. Use a separate piece of paper for your rewrite.

> I was sleeping in my apartment in the Athlete's Village on a quiet Sunday morning. It was the day before my team's soccer match in the 2012 Olympic Games, and I needed my rest. That's when a loud argument awoke me. From my window, I could see that a car had broken down in the middle of the street. The driver had his car's hood raised, as he looked for the problem. The garbage man was angry because he couldn't get his truck by to collect the trash. The driver refused to push his car to the side of the road. A policeman came by to see if he could help. He tried to start the vehicle, and then said, "Looks like you're out of gas, guy." He helped clear the road, and the street became quiet again. I went back to sleep, dreaming of scoring the winning goal.

The Torch Relay

The Olympic flame is one of the most important symbols of the Games. It was originally used as a sign of truce between athletes to put aside the differences of their countries. Each olympiad since 1936, hundreds of people participate in a torch relay to carry the Olympic flame from the site of the Ancient Olympic Games (Olympia, Greece) to the site of the current Olympic Games.

The flame is always carried in a special torch, designed specifically for the current Games. London's 2012 Olympic torch is gold colored and has 8,000 circles (holes). The circles represent the eight thousand torchbearers who were chosen to carry the torch because of their inspiring stories and their contributions to their communities.

London's torch will arrive in the United Kingdom on May 18, 2012. From then until the Opening Ceremonies, the torch will be carried all around the U.K. by those fortunate enough to take part in Olympic history. On the evening of the Opening Ceremonies, one final torchbearer will have the privilege of using the torch to light a special cauldron in Olympic Stadium. The flame in the cauldron will burn continuously until the end of the Closing Ceremonies.

The person chosen to be the final bearer is often an inspirational and symbolic choice. This person usually means a lot to the host country and its people. Here are some past final bearers of the torch:

- **1952—Helsinki, Finland: Paavo Nurmi**
  This Finnish runner was a great past Olympian who had won 12 Olympic medals (9 gold and 3 silver) over three olympiads.

- **1964—Tokyo, Japan: Yoshinori Sakai**
  This 19-year-old Japanese runner was born in Hiroshima on August 6, 1945, the exact day an atomic bomb was dropped on that city during World War II. He was chosen to symbolize peace and the rebuilding of Japan.

- **1976—Montreal, Canada: Sandra Henderson and Stéphane Préfontaine**
  These two Canadian teens were the first pair to light an Olympic cauldron together. Henderson, an English speaker, and Préfontaine, a French speaker, were chosen to symbolize the two founding peoples of Canada.

Activity: If the Olympic Games were being hosted by your city, state, province, or country, who would you want to be the final torchbearer? Would you choose a great Olympian, like Nurmi, or would you choose someone who symbolized peace, like Sakai? Would your choice be symbolic of your place's past and future?

On a separate piece of paper, write about who you would choose to have as the final torchbearer. Explain why you have made this particular choice. Next to your essay, draw a picture of your person or of the special torch that would be used to light the Olympic flame.

Olympic Sports

There will be 26 different sports featured in the 2012 Olympic Games, and some of those sports have several disciplines. (A discipline is a sub-category of the sport that has its own rules.) Below and on pages 28–32 are the descriptions of each Olympic sport.

Activity: As you are reading, imagine what it would be like to compete in each sport. After you have learned about all the sports, pick your favorite one and write creatively. Imagine that you are representing your country in the Olympic Games. Describe one moment in vivid detail. Perhaps while you are walking out into the arena, preparing to compete, or while you are in the middle of your competition. Use sensory details (touch, sound, sight, taste, smell) and describe how you feel. Make your reader feel as if he or she is there, experiencing everything.

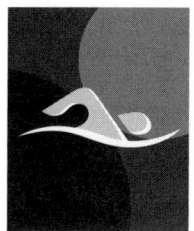

Aquatics   *Olympic Sport Since 1896*

All of the Olympic water sports fall under the category of Aquatics. Many—such as swimming, diving, and water polo—have been part of the Olympic Games for over 100 years. Synchronized swimming—a women-only sport—did not become an official part of the Games until 1984.

Archery   *Olympic Sport Since 1900*

Athletes competing in this sport must have strong hands, sharp eyes, and steady nerves as they use bows to aim their arrows at distant targets. No country has won more gold medals in archery than South Korea (16).

Athletics   *Olympic Sport Since 1896*

The popular sport of athletics features some of the world's greatest athletes. There are four main types of athletics events: track events (short- to medium-distance runs), field events (jumping, throwing), combined events (decathlon, heptathlon), and road events (long-distance runs and walks). In all, there will be 47 total events that fall under the category of Athletics in 2012.

Badminton   *Olympic Sport Since 1992*

Athletes use rackets to hit a shuttlecock (which is made of cork and goose feathers) over a net. The shuttlecock has been clocked at speeds of over 161 miles (260 km) per hour, making badminton the world's fastest racket sport. China, South Korea, and Indonesia combined have won 23 of the 24 Olympic gold medals awarded in this sport.

Olympic Sports

Basketball   *Olympic Sport Since 1936*

In this sport, teams of five battle each other on a hardwood court. The U.S. men's basketball team has taken the gold medal in 13 of the 16 Olympics Games they have competed in.

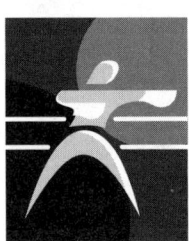

Boxing   *Olympic Sport Since 1904*

This brutal test of speed, strength, stamina, and courage was twice banned from Olympic competition (in 1896 and 1912). The sport's Olympic origins go all the way back to the Ancient Olympic Games.

Canoeing/Kayaking   *Olympic Sport Since 1936*

There are two disciplines in this Olympic sport: sprint and slalom. Sprint racing takes place in lanes on calm waters. In slalom racing, the paddlers must make their way through rough waters.

Cycling   *Olympic Sport Since 1896*

There will be four cycling disciplines in 2012:
1. *BMX:* Also known as *motocross*, BMX has its riders compete on a course that includes jumps and other obstacles.
2. *Road:* Cyclists are timed as they race over long distances.
3. *Track:* Riders race at tremendous speeds around a banked, or angled, track.
4. *Mountain Bike:* Riders maneuver over a hilly course that is covered with such natural obstacles as trees, rocks, branches, and streams.

Equestrian   *Olympic Sport Since 1900*

This is the only Olympic sport in which people compete with the help of animals (though equestrian events are a part of the modern pentathlon). The horse and its rider combine speed, grace, and artistry to complete certain movements, steps, and jumps.

Olympic Sports

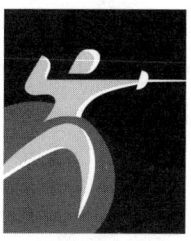

Fencing
Olympic Sport Since 1896

Opponents face off and try to score points on each other with one of three types of weapons. When using a foil, one can score points by striking the opponent's torso. With the épée, one can strike an opponent anywhere on the body. When using a sabre, strikes are restricted to above the waist.

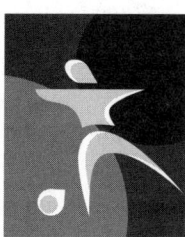

Football (Soccer)
Olympic Sport Since 1900

Widely considered to be the most popular sport in the world, this game pits two teams of 11 players each against each other. Two countries have winning streaks to defend in 2012: the men's team from Argentina and the women's team from the United States each took home the gold medals in both 2004 and 2008.

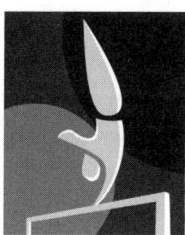

Gymnastics
Olympic Sport Since 1896

Gymnasts combine incredible balance and gracefulness with power and strength to perform challenging routines. In the 2012 Olympic Games, there will be three different disciplines:

1. *Artistic:* Judges give scores for performances in a series of events (floor exercise, pommel horse, rings, vault, parallel bars, and horizontal bar for men; floor exercise, vault, uneven bars, and balance beam for women).

2. *Rhythmic:* This combination of gymnastics and dance is one of only two Olympic disciplines that is competed in by women only. (Synchronized swimming is the other.)

3. *Trampoline:* This discipline, which made its Olympic debut in 2000, involves a series of short routines. Gymnasts twist, bounce, and do somersaults with the aid of a trampoline.

Handball
Olympic Sport Since 1936

In this fast-paced, high-energy game, athletes use their hands to dribble, pass, and catch a small ball. Two teams of seven players each compete to see who can score the most goals.

Olympic Sports

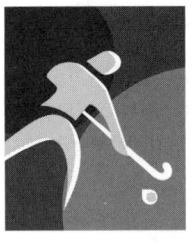

Hockey
Olympic Sport Since 1908

In this ancient game played on grass, athletes use a crooked stick to shoot a small ball into a net. No country has had more Olympic success in this sport than India, winner of eight Olympic gold medals.

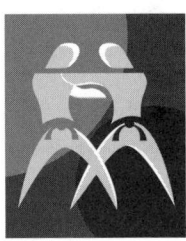

Judo
Olympic Sport Since 1964

Although the word *judo* means "the gentle way" in Japanese, judo is actually an ancient style of hand-to-hand combat. Competitors from Japan have dominated this Olympic Games sport, taking home 35 gold medals. (France comes in second with 10 gold medals earned.)

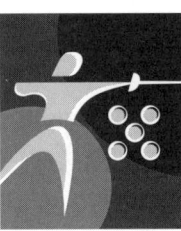

Modern Pentathlon
Olympic Sport Since 1912

The multi-talented athletes of this sport compete in five events. In order, the events are fencing (with an épée, which is the heaviest of the fencing weapons), swimming (200-meter freestyle), show jumping (on horseback), running (3 kilometers) and shooting (with a pistol).

Rowing
Olympic Sport Since 1900

There are two main types of rowing races: sweep oar (where each rower has one oar) and sculling (where each rower has two oars). Each boat contains one, two, four, or eight rowers, depending on the event.

Sailing
Olympic Sport Since 1900

There will be 10 sailing events in 2012. In Olympic sailing, boats of the same class, or design, are raced against each other. As early as 1900, women were a part of some sailing teams, but the first exclusively women's events were not introduced until 1988.

Olympic Sports

Shooting   *Olympic Sport Since 1896*

In the Olympic Games, there are three different types of shooting events: shotgun, rifle, and pistol. Men have competed in this sport since the first Modern Olympic Games in 1896. However, women's shooting events did not become official until 1984.

Table Tennis   *Olympic Sport Since 1988*

Millions of people play this paddle game (also known as Ping-Pong) for fun, but few can compete in the Olympic Games. When players at this level strike the ball, it can travel at speeds of up to 100 miles (160 km) per hour.

Taekwondo   *Olympic Sport Since 2000*

Taekwondo means "the way of kicking and striking," and it is the traditional martial art of Korea. Athletes use their hands and especially their feet to defeat their opponents. There are four weight classes that compete at the Olympic Games (from lightest to heaviest): flyweight, lightweight, middleweight, and heavyweight.

Tennis   *Olympic Sport Since 1896*

This court game can be played in singles matches (one on one) or doubles matches (two on two). In doubles play, the playing area is 9 feet (2.74 meters) wider. Tennis was an official event at the Olympic Games from 1896–1924. It was then dropped for 60 years—appearing only once during that time (in 1968)—before re-emerging in the 1984 Olympic Games.

Triathlon   *Olympic Sport Since 2000*

The triathlon is a combination of three consecutive events: a 1,640 yard (1.5 km) swim, a 24.9-mile (40 km) bike race, and a 6.2-mile (10 km) run. In 2000, the Olympic record holder in this event—Simon Whitfield of Canada—completed all three of these rigorous tests of endurance and stamina in less time than it might take to watch a movie (1 hour, 48 minutes, and 24 seconds)!

Olympic Sports

Volleyball   *Olympic Sport Since 1964*

This Olympic sport is unique in that it can be played on a hardwood court or on a sandy beach. In the court version, each team has six starting players and available substitutes. In beach volleyball, each team is made up of just two people.

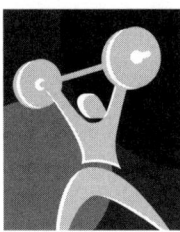

Weightlifting   *Olympic Sport Since 1896*

This sport showcases strength in its purest form. Since the beginning of the Olympic Games, the world's strongest men have competed in this sport, but women's events were not added until 2000. In weightlifting, there are two main types of lifts:

1. *Clean and Jerk:* This type of lift is done in two parts and begins with the athlete pulling the loaded barbell off the ground and bringing the weights up to rest near his or her collarbone area. The lifter then executes the "jerk" part, lifting the barbell up over his or her head.

2. *Snatch:* In this type of lift, the weight is pulled from the ground to overhead in one explosive motion.

Wrestling   *Olympic Sport Since 1896*

This may be the oldest of all competitive sports. For the Olympic Games, wrestling comes in two disciplines:

1. *Greco-Roman:* In this discipline, wrestlers can only use their arms and upper bodies to defeat opponents.

2. *Freestyle:* In this discipline, trips, pushes, and other leg moves are allowed.

Olympic Sports

Directions: Use the information on pages 27 through 32 to complete these challenges.

Bronze-Medal Challenge

Some Olympic sports have several disciplines. Under each sport listed, name its disciplines.

Wrestling	Cycling	Gymnastics

Silver-Medal Challenge

Complete the graph: Of the 26 Olympic sports, 9 were featured in the first Modern Olympic Games of 1896. Shade the bar graph to show when the other 17 sports first became official.

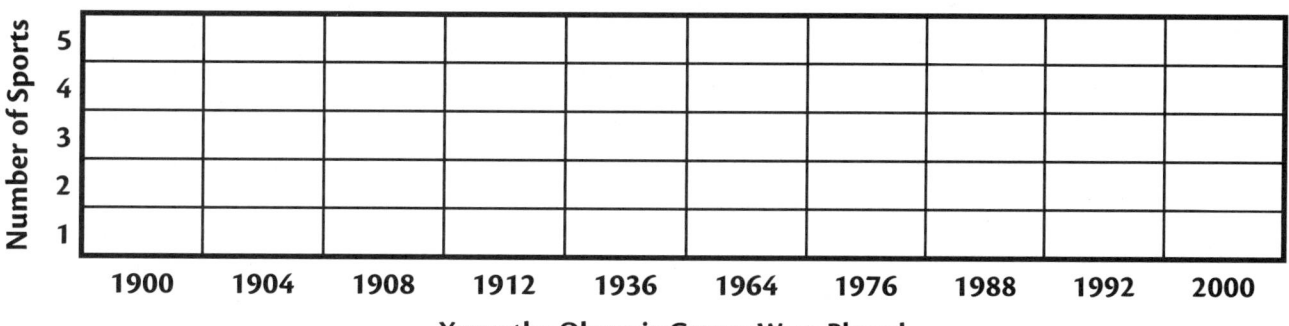

Gold-Medal Challenge

For each math challenge below, circle the correct answer.

a. number of beach-volleyball players in a tournament featuring 12 teams — 24   72   144

b. total number of kilometers (km) a person competing in the triathlon must travel to complete the course — 6.2   35   51.5

c. the year judo became an Olympic sport minus the number of players in a tennis doubles match divided by the number of sailing events in the 2012 Games — 19.60   196.0   1960

The Olympic Program

The 17 days of the London 2012 Olympic Games will be a busy time! With 26 sports played at 30 venues, the Olympic action will be thrilling and constant. Here is the schedule. Study it to see when your favorite sports will be played. Then take the Olympic Program Challenges on page 35.

July/August 2012	27	28	29	30	31	1	2	3	4	5	6	7	8	9	10	11	12
Day	F	S	S	M	T	W	T	F	S	S	M	T	W	T	F	S	S
Opening Ceremonies	■																
Aquatics		■	■	■	■	■	■	■	■	■	■	■	■	■	■	■	
Archery	■	■	■	■	■	■	■	■									
Athletics								■	■	■	■	■	■	■	■	■	■
Badminton		■	■	■	■	■	■	■	■	■							
Basketball		■	■	■	■	■	■	■	■	■	■	■	■	■	■	■	■
Boxing		■	■	■	■	■	■	■	■	■	■	■	■	■	■	■	■
Canoeing/Kayaking			■	■	■	■	■				■	■	■	■	■	■	
Cycling		■	■			■		■				■	■		■	■	
Equestrian		■	■	■		■	■	■			■	■	■	■			
Fencing		■	■	■	■	■	■	■									
Football (Soccer)		■	■		■	■					■			■	■		
Gymnastics		■	■	■	■	■	■	■	■	■	■	■	■	■	■	■	■
Handball		■	■	■	■	■	■	■	■	■	■	■	■	■	■	■	■
Hockey		■	■	■	■	■	■	■	■	■	■	■	■	■	■		
Judo		■	■	■	■	■	■	■									
Modern Pentathlon																■	■
Rowing		■	■	■	■	■	■	■									
Sailing			■	■	■	■	■	■	■	■	■	■	■	■	■		
Shooting		■	■	■	■	■	■	■									
Table Tennis		■	■	■	■	■	■	■	■	■	■	■					
Taekwondo													■	■	■	■	
Tennis		■	■	■	■	■	■	■									
Triathlon									■			■					
Volleyball		■	■	■	■	■	■	■	■	■	■	■	■	■	■	■	■
Weightlifting		■	■	■		■		■	■	■	■	■	■				
Wrestling										■	■	■	■	■	■	■	■
Closing Ceremonies																	■

The Olympic Program

Directions: Use your Olympic Program on page 34 to complete these challenges.

Bronze-Medal Challenge

Answer the following question: Which three sports will be played on both Thursdays but only one Wednesday during the 2012 Olympic Games?

Silver-Medal Challenge

Write how many days each of these sports will be played during the 2012 Olympic Games. Then complete the chart to the right by listing the sports in order. Put the sport that will be played the most at the top of the chart, and so on.

_____ Athletics

_____ Badminton

_____ Cycling

_____ Gymnastics

_____ Judo

_____ Sailing

_____ Volleyball

_____ Wrestling

Gold-Medal Challenge

Use the three pieces of information given to solve each of these problems.

1. This sport requires a racket.

   This sport does not use a round ball.

   This sport will crown its gold-medal winner on Sunday, August 5.

   Which sport is it? _____

2. This date is on a weekday.

   This date is made up of odd numbers.

   On this date, archery and football (soccer) events will be held, but not cycling.

   Which date is it? _____

35

Sports Categories

In total, there will be 26 sports featured in the 2012 Olympic Games. Some of them have things in common with other sports. Some are completely unique. Write down every sport that fits into these categories. (**Hint:** Even if only a part of this sport applies, put it into the category listed.)

Aquatics ✦ Archery ✦ Athletics ✦ Badminton ✦ Basketball ✦ Boxing
Canoeing/Kayaking ✦ Cycling ✦ Equestrian ✦ Fencing ✦ Football ✦ Gymnastics ✦ Handball
Hockey ✦ Judo ✦ Modern Pentathlon ✦ Rowing ✦ Sailing ✦ Shooting ✦ Table Tennis
Taekwondo ✦ Tennis ✦ Triathlon ✦ Volleyball ✦ Weightlifting ✦ Wrestling

Sports Played in Water	**Sports Played on a Court**
Sports Played on a Field	**Sports Played on a Track**
Sports Played on a Horse	**Hand-to-Hand Combat Sports**
Sports That Use a Round Object	**Sports That Use a Pointed Object**

You Make the Choice

In 1896, there were only nine sports scheduled to be a part of the first Modern Olympic Games. By the time of the 2008 Olympic Games, the number had grown to include 28 sports. For the 2012 Games, two sports have been taken off the list.

The International Olympic Committee (IOC) meets each year to make many decisions about the Olympic Games. They choose the host cities, and they also decide which sports should be included on the program.

Now is your chance to state your opinion. Look at pages 27–32 for a list of the 26 sports on the 2012 program. What sports are missing? Are there any that you think should be a part of the Olympic Games? Fill out the form below with a sport that is not currently a part of the Olympic Games. You can pick your favorite sport, or you can create a whole new sport of your own.

Name of the Sport

Uniform	Equipment
Draw here	*Draw here*
Describe here	*Describe here*

How the Sport Is Played

Olympic Ideals

One of the greatest goals of the Olympic Games is to bring out the best in people—not just as athletes, but also as neighbors. Two ideals that illustrate this goal are the Olympic Truce and the Olympic Creed.

The Olympic Truce

The Olympic Games is an event that promotes peace and the breaking down of borders between countries and cultures. But the world is not always a peaceful place. Often, countries are at war with each other. That is why the Olympic Truce is so important. A truce is an agreement to stop fighting.

The Truce began all the way back in the time of the Ancient Olympic Games. It was called *Ekecheiria* back then, and it allowed Greek athletes and citizens to travel to the Games without fear of being attacked. The truce was announced just before the first day of the Games, and it lasted until the athletes had returned home safely. Today, the General Assembly of the United Nations announces the truce one year before the Games begin and asks that all nations recognize its importance.

Do you think the Olympic Truce is less important or more important now than it was back in the time of the Ancient Greeks? Explain your answer.

_____

_____

The Olympic Creed

The Olympic Creed is a standard that all athletes who compete in the Olympic Games try to live up to. This is what it says:

> *"The most important thing in the Olympic Games is not to win, but to take part, just as the most important thing in life is not the triumph but the struggle. The essential thing is not to have conquered but to have fought well."*

List three ways that you think an athlete can honor the Olympic Creed.

1. _____
2. _____
3. _____

Describe one way that you think an athlete could dishonor the Olympic Creed.

_____

_____

Medal of Honor

Every olympiad, hundreds of athletes earn gold, silver, and bronze medals. It is just about the highest honor an Olympian can receive. But there is one medal that only a few Olympians have earned, and that is the Pierre de Coubertin medal. The Pierre de Coubertin medal is also known as the True Spirit of Sportsmanship medal, and it has been awarded only 11 times. Here are two of the stories behind the medal:

Lawrence Lemieux

It was September 24, 1988, and the sailing competition was underway in the waters near Seoul, South Korea, site of the 1988 Olympic Games. The once-peaceful weather suddenly became very windy. A Canadian sailor named Lawrence Lemieux was running in second place when he noticed an emergency occurring on another course. A boat carrying two sailors from Singapore had turned over, injuring the men and dumping them into the water. Lemieux broke away from his race and headed straight for the sailors. He pulled them from the water and waited with them until a patrol boat came. Lemieux then rejoined his race, but he had lost so much time that he ended up in 22nd place.

The International Yacht Racing Union unanimously decided to award Lemieux second place, and the International Olympic Committee (IOC) gave him the Pierre de Coubertin award for displaying such great courage and self-sacrifice.

Vanderlei de Lima

On August 29, 2004 in Athens, Greece, a Brazilian runner named Vanderlei de Lima was in first place in the men's marathon at the Olympic Games. He had a lead of almost 30 seconds. Suddenly, a man jumped out of the crowd and grabbed the runner. He wrestled with him, and knocked him into a group of spectators. When he got free, the marathoner continued on the course, but he had lost valuable time. He was soon passed by two other runners. He earned the bronze medal, but many people felt that he had been robbed of the gold. The Brazilian Track Federation made an appeal so that de Lima could be awarded first place, but the appeal was rejected.

The IOC awarded de Lima the Pierre de Coubertin Award for the sportsmanship and grace he showed in the way he handled the incident. In 2005, a gold-medal-winning Brazilian volleyball player named Emanuel Rego gave de Lima his gold medal on national TV, but de Lima did not accept the medal. He said, "I can't accept Emanuel's medal. I'm happy with mine; it's bronze but means gold."

Activity: Read "Olympic Ideals" on page 38. On a separate piece of paper, answer these questions. Explain each answer fully. Use complete sentences.
- ✦ Do you think Lemieux and de Lima deserved the de Coubertin award?
- ✦ Do you think it was right to award Lemieux second place in the sailing competition?
- ✦ Do you think it was right to deny de Lima the gold medal in the marathon?

The Paralympic Games

In 2012, the city of London will not only be hosting the Olympic Games; it will also be hosting the Paralympic Games. Since 1960, athletes with disabilities have competed in the Paralympic Games. The word *paralympic* is a combination of the Greek affix *para*, which means "alongside" or "beside" and the word *Olympics*. The athletes who qualify for the Paralympic Games have disabilities, such as the following:

- blindness or visual impairment
- cerebral palsy
- intellectual disability
- spinal injury
- amputation (having part or all of a limb removed)
- "les autres" or *the others*, disabilities that don't fall into the other categories

Though the Paralympic Games weren't officially held until 1960, the beginnings of this event can be traced back to 1948. Back then, an English doctor from Stoke Mandeville Hospital named Ludwig Guttman felt that competition would be helpful in rehabilitating the many soldiers who were severely injured on the battlegrounds of World War II. He helped organize physical competitions between patients, and these early competitions were referred to as the Stoke Mandeville Games. It is from this that 2012 Paralympic mascot Mandeville gets its name.

From those beginnings, the Paralympic Games has grown into a huge international event with thousands of athletes competing in several sports. In 2012, Paralympic athletes will compete in 20 different sports:

Archery ✦ Goalball ✦ Table Tennis ✦ Athletics ✦ Judo
Volleyball–Sitting ✦ Boccia ✦ Powerlifting ✦ Wheelchair Basketball ✦ Cycling ✦ Rowing
Wheelchair Fencing ✦ Equestrian ✦ Sailing ✦ Wheelchair Rugby ✦ Football 5-a-side
Shooting ✦ Wheelchair Tennis ✦ Football 7-a-side ✦ Swimming

Activity: Pick a sport and create a compare-and-contrast chart. On the left side, list all of the things that Olympic athletes and Paralympic athletes have in common. On the right side, list all of the special challenges that Paralympic athletes face as they compete in this sport.

(Go to *http://www.london2012.com/games/index.php* and click on the "Paralympic sports" tab to find out more about your chosen sport.)

Things in Common	Differences

Sample Chart

Paralympic Greats

Just as there have been special athletes who have shone throughout Olympic Games history, there have also been Paralympic greats whose feats are legendary. Here are a few of those amazing athletes:

No one has won more Paralympic medals than **Trischa Zorn**. Blind from birth, this swimmer from the United States competed in her first Paralympic Games in 1980 and her last in 2004. Over that span, she earned 55 total Paralympic medals, 41 of which were gold. Following the 2000 Games, she was the world record holder in eight swimming categories.

While Zorn can be said to be the most successful of the Paralympic athletes, perhaps none are more famous than **Oscar Pistorius**. A double amputee runner from South Africa, Pistorius is known as "the fastest man on no legs." Pistorius was born missing bones in his lower legs; and before he turned one, both legs were amputated below the knees. Through the use of artificial lower legs, Pistorius grew to be an incredible athlete who excelled at rugby, tennis, and water polo. He actually didn't begin training as a runner until January of 2004, but he qualified for the Paralympic Games in September of that year! He took the 2004 Games by storm, breaking the world record in the 200-meter run even though he was competing against athletes who had only one artificial leg. In 2008, Pistorius tried to qualify for the able-bodied Olympic Games, but was just seven-tenths of a second too slow to meet the requirement. Instead, he went on to win three gold medals at the 2008 Paralympic Games.

Though Pistorius was not able to fulfill his dream of competing in the Olympic Games, a paraplegic archer from New Zealand named **Neroli Fairhall** did accomplish that feat. In 1984, Fairhall became the first Paralympic athlete to compete in the able-bodied Games. She placed 35th in the Olympic competition. That same year, she took home the gold in Paralympic archery.

Activity: Fill in the circle next to the correct answer.

1. How many of the Paralympic medals that Trischa Zorn won were silver or bronze?

    Ⓐ 55   Ⓑ 41   Ⓒ 14   Ⓓ 34

2. How close was Oscar Pistorius to qualifying for the able-bodied Olympics in 2008?

    Ⓐ .07 seconds   Ⓑ .70 seconds   Ⓒ .007 seconds   Ⓓ 7.10 seconds

3. In 1984, how many athletes did better in Paralympic archery competition than Neroli Fairhall?

    Ⓐ 33   Ⓑ 34   Ⓒ 1   Ⓓ 0

The Olympic Mascots

For each Olympiad, the host city creates mascots that give a fun face to the Olympic Games. For 2012, London has created two mascots: Wenlock and Mandeville. The story goes that these two mascots were created from the last two drops of shiny steel used to build Olympic Stadium in London. Their shininess allows them to reflect the faces and places they meet as they travel around London. Each mascot also has a camera lens for an eye, which lets them capture everything they see. Here are a few more details about these adventurous creations:

✦ **Wenlock** is the official mascot of the 2012 Olympic Games. Wenlock gets its name from a town where Olympic-style competitions were held in the 19th century. The five bracelets on Wenlock's arm are the five colors of the Olympic rings. Wenlock loves meeting people and being positive, and his main mission is to do his best and help others do their best, too. This is why Wenlock has three points on his head to represent the three places on the podium where Olympic winners stand.

✦ **Mandeville** is the official mascot of the 2012 Paralympic Games. Mandeville gets its name from the town where Sir Ludwig Guttman held a competition in 1948 for World War II soldiers who had suffered spinal injuries. Mandeville has a sleek, aerodynamic head and a timer on his wrist. This is because he's always on the go. Mandeville likes to push himself to do better and better in everything he does. He feels this captures the spirit of the Paralympic Games and the athletes who compete in them.

For more on Wenlock and Mandeville, visit *www.mylondon2012.com/mascots/*.

Directions: Imagine your city is hosting the Olympic Games. Create a mascot that could represent both your city and the Games. On the lines below, write a description of your mascot. Then, draw a picture of it in the box. Don't forget to give your creation a name!

Another Idea: Choose a city, state, or place other than your city. The place you choose can be ridiculous or even fictional (made up). Just be sure to tell why the mascot you have created would be a good representation of your place and the Olympic Games.

Mascot Name

The Athlete's Room

In preparation for the 2012 Olympic Games, a state-of-the-art Athletes' Village has been built in the middle of London. This village will house over 17,000 athletes and officials. Each room will feature wireless Internet service and a view of beautiful Olympic Park.

Directions: Imagine you are an athlete who has been assigned a room in the Athletes' Village. You can furnish your room in any way you see fit, but you have a limited amount of money and space. Look at the list of items below. Each comes with its dimensions and its cost listed. How good of a bargain shopper are you? What are the most important items for you to have? Draw in your items on the room to the left and list your purchases on the form to the right. Here are the rules:

✦ You have $100 in Olympic Bucks to spend. You can buy as many things (and as many of each thing) as you want, but you cannot go over budget.

✦ Each square in the room equals 1 square foot (sq. ft.). Remember to leave space for walkways in your room!

Item	Cost	Sq. Feet	Item	Cost	Sq. Feet
Bed	$26	3 x 6	Table Tennis Table	$13	3 x 5
Comfy Chair	$16	2 x 2	Portable Fan	$5	1 x 1
Flat-Screen TV	$36	2 x 1	Small Sofa	$13	4 x 2
Exercise Treadmill	$10	2 x 3	Small Table	$7	3 x 3
Older TV with Stand	$17	2 x 3	Vending Machine	$11	3 x 3

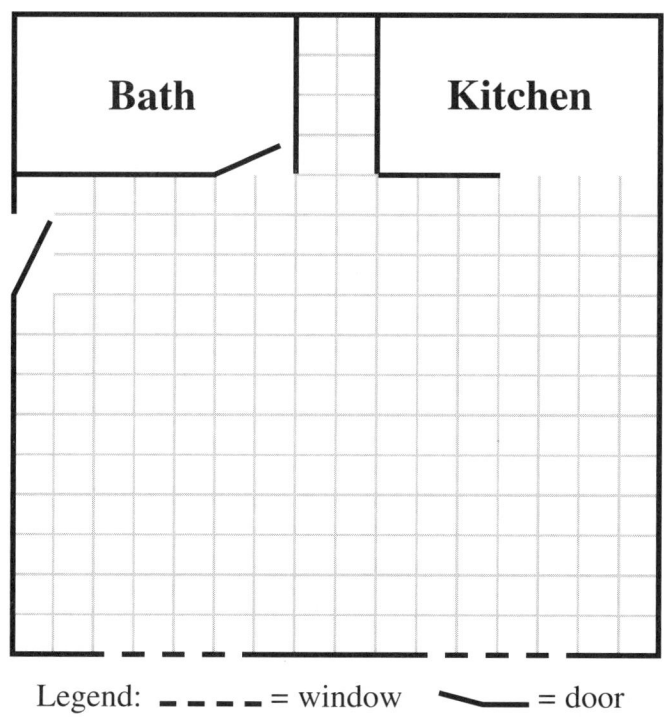

Legend: - - - - = window   ⌒ = door

Item Purchased	Amount
Total Spent:	

Five-Day Forecast

Imagine you are visiting London for the 2012 Olympic Games. You will want to know what the weather will be like so you can pack the correct clothing. You've heard that London weather is often gloomy and sometimes rainy, but you decide to look online for the upcoming forecast. That's when you see that the weather will be 30°! That sounds way too cold for running and swimming and field hockey. Doesn't water freeze at 32°?

Water does, in fact, freeze at 32°—but only if you are using the Fahrenheit (F) scale. That's the way of measuring temperature that is used primarily in the United States. But many other countries, including England, use the Celsius (C) scale. On that scale, water freezes at 0° and boils at 100°.

So what does it mean when it says that the weather will be 30°C. Is that warm or cold? What you need is a way to convert Celsius temperatures to Fahrenheit.

To convert Celsius temperatures to Fahrenheit:
1. Multiply the Celsius temperature by 9.
2. Then divide by 5.
3. Then add 32 to the result.

Example: To convert 30°C to Fahrenheit, 30 x 9 = 270
270 ÷ 5 = 54; 54 + 32 = 86. Therefore, 30°C = 86°F.

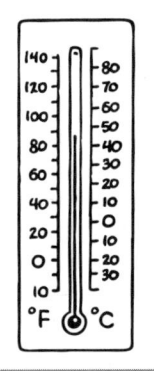

Now look at the five-day forecast below. You've been given the temperature in Celsius. Use a piece of scratch paper to calculate each temperature in Fahrenheit and write your answers on the lines. Round your answers up or down to the nearest degree.

Monday 26°C	Tuesday 24°C	Wednesday 31°C	Thursday 25°C	Friday 27°C
____ °F	____ °F	____ °F	____ °F	____ °F
Clear Skies	Windy	Sunny	Cloudy	Clear Skies

44

The Metric System

Just as with measuring temperature, the United States uses a different system of measuring distance, length, and weight than most of the rest of the world. The United States uses the U.S. customary system, while countries such as England use the metric system. For all Olympic Games, even those hosted by U.S. cities, the metric system is used.

Directions: Solve the measurement conversion problems below. All you need is the Metric Conversion Chart and some scratch paper or a calculator. Round your answers to the nearest whole number.

Metric Conversion Chart

Distance, Height, and Length
1 centimeter = .4 inches or .03 feet
1 meter = 39.4 inches or 3.3 feet
 or 1.1 yards
1 kilometer = .6 miles

Weight
1 gram = .04 ounces
1 kilogram = 2.2 pounds

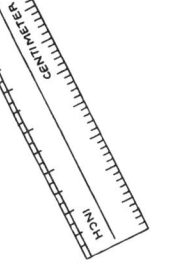

1. The Olympic and world record for most weight lifted in the clean and jerk competition is 263.5 kilograms.

   263.5 kilograms = _____ pounds

2. The bullseye (center) on an archery target can be as small as 40 cm across.

   40 centimeters = _____ inches

3. The winner of the men's 100-meter race is often called "World's Fastest Man."

   100 meters = _____ yards

4. In road cycling, women race on a course that is over 120 kilometers long.

   120 kilometers = _____ miles

5. Football (soccer) games take place on a 105 m by 68 m playing field.

   105 meters long by 68 meters wide = _____ yards long by _____ yards wide

Challenge: Using your answers to question #5, what is the perimeter of the playing field in a football (soccer) game? What is the area? Give your answers in yards.

Perimeter: _____ Area: _____

45

2012 Analogies

Directions: Complete the following analogies about all things London and the 2012 Olympic Games.

1. U.S. customary system : ounces :: metric system :

   Ⓐ inches   Ⓑ pounds   Ⓒ grams   Ⓓ tonnes

2. Modern Olympic Games : gold medal :: Ancient Olympic Games :

   Ⓐ torch   Ⓑ sabre   Ⓒ bronze medal   Ⓓ olive wreath

3. BMX : cycling :: Greco-Roman :

   Ⓐ boxing   Ⓑ wrestling   Ⓒ judo   Ⓓ taekwondo

4. gasoline : petrol :: cookies :

   Ⓐ bobbies   Ⓑ biscuits   Ⓒ bonnets   Ⓓ blokes

5. United States : Congress :: United Kingdom :

   Ⓐ Queen   Ⓑ Royal Family   Ⓒ Duke   Ⓓ Parliament

6. archery : bow :: fencing :

   Ⓐ épée   Ⓑ pistol   Ⓒ judo   Ⓓ shuttlecock

7. 2012 : London :: 2016 :

   Ⓐ Athens   Ⓑ Paris   Ⓒ Chicago   Ⓓ Rio de Janeiro

8. Olympic Games : Wenlock :: Paralympic Games :

   Ⓐ Mandeville   Ⓑ Guttman   Ⓒ de Coubertin   Ⓓ Spyridon

Keep Track in 2012

Directions: Keep up with all of the action and excitement of the 2012 Olympic Games. Choose five countries and use tally marks to record each medal that those countries earn.

Country	Gold	Silver	Bronze	Total

Answer Key

Ancient Olympic Games (page 4)
1. Ancient
2. Modern
3. Modern
4. Ancient
5. Modern
6. Ancient
7. Modern
8. Ancient and Modern
9. Modern
10. Ancient and Modern

Modern Olympic Games (page 7)
Bronze-Medal Challenge: a. John and Sumner Paine, American; b. Spyridon Louis, Greek; c. Pierre de Coubertin, French
Silver-Medal Challenge: 4, 1, 5, 2, 3
Gold-Medal Challenge: a. Qatar; b. weightlifting, highlights; c. Olympic-style, large-scale, all-male, second-place; d. 10,000; e. international; f. debate

The Host Cities (page 9)
Bronze-Medal Challenge: July 19; 1952, 1980, 1996
Silver-Medal Challenge: 1. The Olympic Games began on November 22 in 1956. 2. The 1956 Olympic Games took place in Melbourne. Australia is in the Southern Hemisphere where the summer months occur later in the year.
Gold-Medal Challenge:

Letter	Continent
C	Asia
B	Australia
D	Europe
A	North America

Map of the British Isles (page 13)

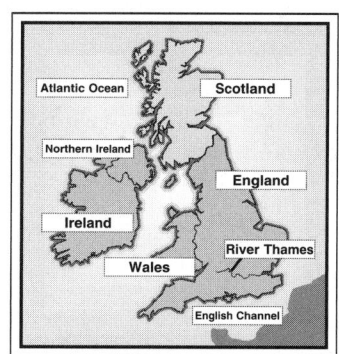

A Place By Any Other Name (page 14)
1. A, B, C, D
2. A
3. A, B, C
4. A, B
5. A, B, C, D

The Royal Family Tree (page 17)
Bronze-Medal Challenge: Victoria—1; Edward VII—5; George V—3; Edward VIII—6; George VI—4; Elizabeth II—2
Silver-Medal Challenge: Diana Spencer — Prince Charles; Wallis Simpson — Edward VIII; Catherine Middleton — Prince William; Lady Elizabeth — George VI; Prince Albert — Queen Victoria
Gold-Medal Challenge: 1. 9 x 5 = 45; 2. 45 – 41 = 4; 3. 4 + 30 = 34

Answer Key

Touring London (page 20)
Bronze-Medal Challenge: D, 800
Silver-Medal Challenge: "The world's first . . ." (C, 1890); "The Great Fire . . ." (B, 1666); "Work is completed . . ." (D, 1994); "The Crown Jewels . . ." (A, 1303)
Gold-Medal Challenge: The London Eye; because it, like Box A, is the tallest of the three

"Site" Seeing (page 21)
Buckingham Palace: black hats, red coats
The London Eye: C, a jelly bean
The London Underground: Each student drawing should include a circle with a horizontal bar over it.
Shakespeare's Globe: 3
The Shard: B, pyramid

Where You're Standing (page 23)
1. A, D
2. A, C
3. A, D
4. B, D
5. A, C
6. A, D
7. A, C
8. A, D
9. B, C
10. A, C, D

Speaking "English" (page 25)
Bronze-Medal Challenge: A: Mandarin Chinese, Spanish, English; B: English, Mandarin Chinese, Spanish
Silver-Medal Challenge: 1. traveller, 2. cruelest, 3. theatre, 4. colour, 5. organize
Gold-Medal Challenge:
I was sleeping in my <u>flat</u> in the Athlete's Village on a quiet Sunday morning. It was the day before my team's <u>football</u> match in the 2012 Olympic Games, and I needed my rest. That's when a loud <u>row</u> awoke me. From my window, I could see that a car had broken down in the middle of the street. The driver had his car's <u>bonnet</u> raised, as he looked for the problem. The <u>dustman</u> was angry because he couldn't get his <u>lorry</u> by to collect the <u>rubbish</u>. The driver refused to push his car to the side of the road. A <u>bobby</u> came by to see if he could help. He tried to start the vehicle, and then said, "Looks like you're out of <u>petrol</u>, <u>bloke</u>." He helped clear the road, and the street became quiet again. I went back to sleep, dreaming of scoring the winning goal.

Olympic Sports (page 33)
Bronze-Medal Challenge: Cycling, 4 (BMX, Road, Track, Mountain Bike); Gymnastics, 3 (Artistic, Rhythmic, Trampoline); Wrestling, 2 (Greco-Roman, Freestyle)
Silver-Medal Challenge:

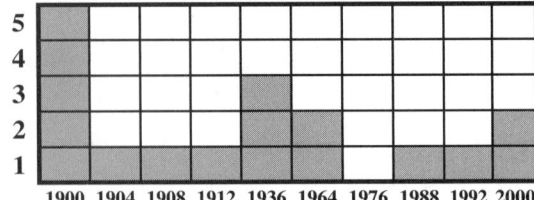

Gold-Medal Challenge: a. 24; b. 51.5; c. 196.0

The Olympic Program (page 35)
Bronze-Medal Challenge: Cycling, Equestrian, Gymnastics
Silver-Medal Challenge: 1. Volleyball (16 days); 2. Gymnastics (15 days); 3. Sailing (14 days); 4. Cycling (13 days); 5. Athletics (10 days); 6. Badminton (9 days); 7. Wrestling (8 days); 8. Judo (7 days)
Gold-Medal Challenge: 1. Badminton; 2. Tuesday, July 31

Sports Categories (page 36)
Possible answers include:
In Water: aquatics, canoeing/kayaking, rowing, sailing, modern pentathlon (swimming), triathlon (swimming)
On a Court: badminton, basketball, handball, tennis, volleyball
On a Field: football, hockey
On a Track: athletics, cycling, modern pentathlon (running)
On a Horse: equestrian, modern pentathlon (horse jumping)
Hand-to-Hand Combat: boxing, judo, taekwondo, wrestling
Use a Round Object: aquatics (water polo), athletics (shot put), basketball, cycling (wheel), football (soccer), handball, hockey, table tennis, tennis, volleyball
Use a Pointed Object: archery (arrow), athletics (javelin), fencing, modern pentathlon (fencing)

Paralympic Greats (page 41)
1. C   2. B   3. D

The Athlete's Room (page 43)
Answers will vary. Check students' work to make sure they did not overspend ($100 or less) and that their purchased furniture fit and was arranged practically.

Five-Day Forecast (page 44)
Monday: 79°F   Wednesday: 88°F   Friday: 81°F
Tuesday: 75°F   Thursday: 77°F

The Metric System (page 45)
1. 580 pounds
2. 16 inches
3. 110 yards
4. 72 miles
5. 116 yards by 75 yards

Challenge: Perimeter = 382 yds.; Area = 8,700 square yds.

2012 Analogies (page 46)
1. C   3. B   5. D   7. D
2. D   4. B   6. A   8. A

> **Internet Research Sites**
> For more information on the London 2012 Olympic Games, visit these websites:
> - www.london2012.com
> - www.teamusa.org
> - www.olympic.org